# Beetles

## Trudi Strain Trueit

Cavendish
Square

New York

Published in 2014 by Cavendish Square Publishing, LLC
303 Park Avenue South, Suite 1247, New York, NY 10010

Website: cavendishsq.com

This publication represents the opinions and views of the author based on his or her personal experience, knowledge, and research. The information in this book serves as a general guide only. The author and publisher have used their best efforts in preparing this book and disclaim liability rising directly or indirectly from the use and application of this book.

CPSIA Compliance Information: Batch #WS13CSQ

All websites were available and accurate when this book was sent to press.

Library of Congress Cataloging-in-Publication Data

Trueit, Trudi Strain.
Beetles / Trudi Strain Trueit.
p. cm. — (Backyard safari)
Includes bibliographical references and index.
Summary: "Identify specific beetles. Explore their behavior, life cycle, mating habits, geographical location, anatomy, enemies, and defenses"—Provided by publisher.
ISBN 978-1-60870-241-1 (hardcover) • ISBN 978-1-62712-027-2 (paperback) • ISBN 978-1-60870-817-8 (ebook)
1. Beetles—Juvenile literature. I. Title.
QL576.2.T78 2013
595.76—dc23
2011036030

Editor: Christine Florie
Art Director: Anahid Hamparian
Series Designer: Alicia Mikles

Expert Reader: Michael Goodrich, professor emeritus, Department of Biological Sciences, Eastern Illinois University, Charleston, Illinois

Photo research by Marybeth Kavanagh

Cover photo by Visuals Unlimited, Inc./Alex Wild/Getty Images
The photographs in this book are used by permission and through the courtesy of: *Getty Images*: Daniel Bosler/Stone, 4; Visuals Unlimited, Inc./Alex Wild, 21; David Wrobel/Visuals Unlimited, Inc., 23BR; *SuperStock*: Mark Cassino, 5; age fotostock, 6, 23TL; Science Faction, 8; Juniors, 9; NHPA, 12, 22BL; Clarence Holmes/age fotostock, 14; Hemis.fr, 16; Blend Images, 19; Minden Pictures, 22TR, 25; imagebroker.net, 22CL, 23CL; Animals Animals, 22CR, 22BR; *Photo Researchers, Inc.*: Nature's Images, 7; *Corbis*: George Grall/National Geographic Society, 10; Alex Wild/Visuals Unlimited, 22TL; *Media Bakery*: BigStockPhoto, 13(hat), 13 (glasses); Veer, 13(brushes); *Cutcaster*: Marek Kosmal, 13(magnifying glass); Sergej Razvodovskij, 13(pencils); *Alamy*: blickwinkel, 15; Marvin Dembinsky Photo Associates, 23TR; Juniors Bildarchiv, 23CR; Nigel Cattlin, 23BL; Bubbles Photolibrary, 26

Printed in the United States of America

# Contents

Introduction    4

**ONE** Beetle World    5

**TWO** You Are the Explorer    12

**THREE** A Guide to Beetles    20

**FOUR** Try This! Projects You Can Do    24

Glossary    29

Find Out More    30

Index    31

# Introduction

Have you ever watched baby spiders hatch from a silky egg sac? Or seen a butterfly sip nectar from a flower? If you have, you know how wonderful it is to discover nature for yourself. Each book in the Backyard Safari series takes you step-by-step on an easy outdoor adventure, then helps you identify the animals you've found. You'll also learn ways to attract, observe, and protect these valuable creatures. As you read, be on the lookout for the Safari Tips and Trek Talk facts sprinkled throughout the book. Ready? The fun starts just steps from your back door!

# ONE
# Beetle World

Has a ladybug ever landed on you? Legend has it that a visit from one of these winged insects brings a person good luck.

Beetles have lived on Earth since before the dinosaurs! Today, there are more than 350,000 known types of beetles on the planet. Scientists figure there are millions more out there waiting to be discovered. Perhaps you will be the one to uncover a beetle no one has ever before seen.

**Trek Talk**
Ladybugs, also called ladybird beetles, may be red, orange, yellow, pink, or black. They can have anywhere from zero to twenty-four spots!

# Life Cycle

Like their insect cousins, butterflies and ants, beetles go through four stages of life: egg, **larva**, **pupa**, and adult.

A female beetle lays one or more eggs. It may lay them on the bottom of a leaf or under the soil. It may also lay them inside things, such as in seeds, wood, or **dung**. The beetle chooses a place where its offspring will have plenty of food to eat as soon as they are born.

**Trek Talk**
A tumblebug rolls dung into a ball, buries it, and lays an egg inside!

A poplar leaf beetle lays eggs. A female beetle can lay thousands of eggs during its lifetime.

This convergent ladybug larva will keep eating and shedding its skin until it enters the pupa stage.

When it is born, a beetle larva looks like a teeny worm. Ladybug larvae look like tiny, mostly black alligators with red or orange markings. A larva cannot do much but eat and grow. As it gets larger, the larva sheds its skin several times. Typically, beetles will stay in the larval stage for a few weeks. Some click beetles may remain larvae for up to three years!

When it is fully grown, a larva releases silky threads. It wraps these threads around itself to form a protective layer, or **cocoon**. The beetle becomes a pupa. During this stage, the insect remains still. Cells break down the body and rebuild it into an adult. Wings, antennae, and adult legs and feet soon form.

An adult beetle breaks free of its cocoon. It is soft and pale. It takes a few minutes for the insect's wings to expand to full size. In a few hours, the beetle's colors darken, and its **exoskeleton** hardens.

A soldier beetle is seen in its pupa stage (left) and as an adult (right).

## Beetle Bodies

Beetles belong to an order of insects called Coleoptera (KOH-lee-AWP-teh-ruh). It means "sheath winged." Most beetles have a pair of hard front wing covers called **elytra**. The elytra protect the two hind wings (not all beetles have hind wings). Hind wings are used for flight. To fly, a beetle opens its elytra, unfolds its hind wings, and hops into the air.

A dung beetle's elytra and hind wings can be seen as it takes flight.

Beetles have three main body parts: head, thorax, and abdomen. The head has eyes, antennae, and mouthparts. Beetles have two eyes, which are made up of many smaller lenses. These compound eyes allow beetles to see in many different directions at once.

Beetles use their antennae for tasting, smelling, touching, balance, and communication. Beetles "talk" to each other by releasing natural chemicals called **pheromones**. Each chemical sends out a different message, such as "I've found food" or "Danger! Stay away." Antennae are used to pick up these chemical messages.

Beetles come in a variety of shapes, sizes, and colors. However, they all share the same body parts.

Beetles have chewing mouthparts that work side to side (humans chew up and down). They have upper and lower lips, back jaws, and strong front jaws called **mandibles**. Beetles that sip the **nectar** from flowers also have tubelike mouthparts similar to drinking straws. Each type of beetle has its favorite foods. Many beetles feast on the flowers, leaves, stems, and roots of plants. Some eat living or dead insects, snails, insect eggs, or worms. Dung beetles and tumblebugs eat animal waste.

Beetles can handle almost any climate, except the bitter cold of Antarctica and the Arctic. You'll find them in hot deserts, mossy swamps, and, probably, your backyard. Are you ready to try to discover some beetles for yourself? It's time to go on safari.

# TWO

# You Are the Explorer

Did you know that one of out every three insects in the world is a beetle? So chances are good that you'll find beetles on your expedition. Still, it helps to know where, when, and how to look for these creatures.

You can go on a beetle safari just about any time of year, though warmer weather will likely give you better results. Choose a mostly sunny day when the temperature is above 60 degrees. If you go after a rainstorm, when the soil is damp, you will probably find beetles close to the surface of the ground.

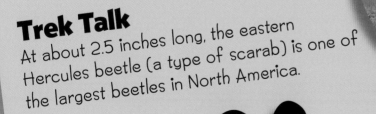

**Trek Talk**
At about 2.5 inches long, the eastern Hercules beetle (a type of scarab) is one of the largest beetles in North America.

# What Do I Wear?

- ❋ A hat with a brim
- ❋ A long-sleeved shirt
- ❋ Jeans or long pants
- ❋ Sunglasses
- ❋ Sunscreen

# What Do I Take?

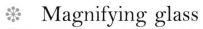

- ❋ Magnifying glass
- ❋ Small paintbrush
- ❋ Plastic spoon
- ❋ Small, clear container
- ❋ Digital camera
- ❋ Notebook
- ❋ Colored pens or pencils

# Where Do I Go?

Beetles will be most attracted to these things in your backyard:

* Flowers
* Vegetables
* Fruit trees
* Dead trees, stumps, or logs
* Wood chips or mulch
* Compost piles
* Grassy or mossy areas
* Flat rocks, loose paver stones, or stepping stones

If your backyard doesn't offer these features, here are some other safari locations you can try:

* Meadows
* Woodlands
* Fields
* Garden nurseries
* Public parks

Always have an adult with you if you are going beyond your backyard.

**Safari Tip**

Looking for ladybugs? Head for the vegetable garden or rosebushes (watch out for the thorns!). Ladybugs eat aphids (AY-fids) and other small insects that suck the juices from plants. Ladybugs are beneficial, or good, insects, because most dine on destructive aphids and not your plants. An adult ladybug may eat up to fifty aphids a day!

A magnifying glass is a good tool to use when looking for beetles.

## What Do I Do?

❋ Use your magnifying glass to help in your search for beetles. Get on your knees, and peer between the blades of grass. Look on flowers, leaves, and trees. Carefully scan porches, patios, and concrete steps. Dig a few inches into wood chips or compost (beetles are good diggers). Also, check under small logs, flat rocks, and paver stones. Many types of ground beetles rest under these things during the day and are active at night.

❋ If you have a dead tree, stump, or log, pull off some loose bark to see if any beetles are inside. Many types of beetles, such as long-horned beetles, snout beetles, and scarabs, eat decaying wood.

* Do you have a vegetable garden? If so, you probably have beetles, too. Cabbage, corn, potatoes, tomatoes, beans, and strawberries are a few of their favorite foods.

* If you discover a beetle, it's best not to touch it. Some beetles bite when threatened. The bombardier beetle gives off a puff of nasty gas to scare away predators. Blister beetles release a liquid from their leg joints that may cause your skin to blister.

* Snap a photo or make a sketch of any beetles you find.

* Make a brief entry in your notebook, too. Describe the beetle. What color is it? Does it have spots, stripes, or other identifying **field marks**? How about a particular feature that stands out, such as long antennae or a large horn on its head? Where did you find the beetle? What was it doing? Leave a blank line on the bottom of the entry to add its name later.

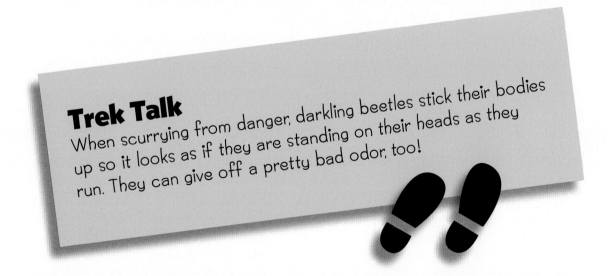

**Trek Talk**

When scurrying from danger, darkling beetles stick their bodies up so it looks as if they are standing on their heads as they run. They can give off a pretty bad odor, too!

BEETLE

Color(s): shiny, dark red and green

Shape: oval

Features: short, bent antennae

Location: peach tree

Activity: eating leaf

Insect name: _____

Your Drawing or
Photo Goes Here

❉ If you want, gently scoot the beetle onto the spoon with your
paintbrush. Put the beetle in the plastic container you brought.
Use your magnifying glass to get a closer look. Pay special
attention to the size and shape of its antennae, which may help
you to identify it. Be sure to write down the description in your
notebook. After a few minutes, carefully place the beetle back
where you found it.

When you find a beetle, gently place it in a clear container for a closer look.

❋ Spend about a half hour to an hour on safari.
❋ Clean up the area, and take everything with you when you leave.

Did you see some different types of beetles on your safari? If so, congratulations! If not, don't worry. Every safari is different. You are sure to have more success on your next adventure. Plan to go on safari again soon. At home, transfer your photos onto the computer and print them. It's time to learn more about your backyard visitors!

# THREE
# A Guide to Beetles

Would you be surprised to learn you are about to begin the most difficult part of your safari? With more than 30,000 different kinds of beetles in North America, identifying what you find can often be the most challenging part of the adventure. Let's try!

Here is what you'll do. Select an entry from your notebook. If you took a photo, now is the time to paste it next to its description. Take a good look at your entry. Ask yourself these questions:

✳ What do the beetle's antennae look like? Are they short or long? Are they threadlike, clubbed, saw-toothed, or bent like an elbow?

✳ What is the shape of the beetle's body? Is it long or short? Rectangular, circular, or oval?

✳ Is the body made up of one color or many colors? Does it have spots, stripes, or other field markings?

✳ Does the beetle have a feature that stands out, such as a long snout (weevil), a horn (a rhinoceros beetle), very long antennae (a long-horned beetle), or large mandibles (a stag beetle)?

Compare the characteristics of your insect with those in the photo guide on pages 22–23. Here's a helpful hint: the largest family of beetles in North America is the rove beetle group, followed by snouts, ground beetles, and leaf beetles. Once you find a match, write its name or family name beside its entry in your notebook.

BEETLE

Color(s): shiny, dark red and green

Shape: oval

Features: short, bent antennae

Location: peach tree

Activity: eating leaf

Insect name: Japanese beetle

If nothing in the photo guide looks familiar, don't get discouraged. There are more than one hundred beetle families in North America—far too many to include here. Look to the resources in the Find Out More section for more help in identifying your beetles.

# Beetle Guide

## BLISTER BEETLES

Spotted Blister Beetle

Striped Blister Beetle

## LADY BEETLES

Seven-Spotted Lady Beetle

Convergent Lady Beetle

## LEAF BEETLES

Asparagus Beetle

Striped Cucumber Beetle

# Beetle Guide

## LONG-HORNED BEETLES

Locust Borer Beetle

Red Milkweed Beetle

## SCARAB BEETLES

Rhinoceros Beetle

Tumblebug

## SNOUT BEETLES

Boll Weevil

Hollyhock Weevil

# FOUR

# Try This!
# Projects You Can Do

Earth would not be the same without beetles. Beetles help to spread plant **pollen** so that new flowers and trees may grow. Many beetles feed on insects, snails, slugs, and other animals that damage plants. Some types, like scarabs, are nature's recyclers. They eat dung, dead plants, and **carrion**.

However, beetles may also be pests. They can spell disaster for farmers trying to grow food for humans. An invasion of beetles can wipe out entire fields of cabbage, beans, corn, wheat, and potatoes in a single season. Here are a few projects you can do to observe beetles and help tip the scales in favor of those that are good for the environment.

## Trek Talk

In ancient Egypt, scarabs were important symbols of life and rebirth. They were often carved out of beautiful stones, such as onyx or lapis lazuli, then placed in tombs to protect the dead in the afterlife.

# Go to the Light

Many beetles, including ground beetles, scarabs, and rove beetles, are attracted to bright light. On a warm evening, just after sunset, turn on your porch light. Watch to see the different types of beetles that come to your light. Write in your notebook about the beetles you observe, and try to identify them. If you live in an area with lightning bugs, be on the lookout for these glowing nighttime fliers. Always have an adult with you, or get permission to be outside after dark.

## Look for the Night Lights

Have you ever seen a lightning bug, or firefly, flicker on a summer night? These beetles have **luminescent** (loo-muh-NESS-ent) glands in their abdomens, which produce light. The larvae are often called glowworms. Adults use their lights to find mates. At night, males take flight, while females remain on the ground. A male will "flash" every five seconds until a female on the ground flashes in return. North America is home to more than 130 different kinds of lightning bugs.

# Ladybug Garden

Did you know a ladybug will fly hundreds of miles in search of food? You can bring ladybugs to your backyard by creating a small garden that attracts the aphids and the scale insects that ladybugs like to eat. Choose six to eight plants from the Ladybug Favorites list on page 27. Your local garden nursery can also help you in selecting the right plants.

Plant a ladybug garden in your backyard, and see how many it attracts!

# Ladybug Favorites Plant List

| FLOWERS | HERBS |
| --- | --- |
| aster | chives |
| cosmos | cilantro |
| marigold | dill |
| nasturtium | fennel |
| rose | lavender |
| sunflower | parsley |

Pick a sunny spot for your garden. Use good soil. Add a few small, flat rocks for the beetles' shelter and **basking**. Water the plants every few days. Never use pesticides. They will kill the ladybugs as well as the insects that the ladybugs dine on. Because ladybugs lay their eggs on their favorite plants, your garden will help keep the ladybug life cycle in motion. Good luck!

## Ladybug House

Ladybugs live for about one year. During the winter, they seek out warm places to stay, such as under rocks, leaves, or bark. Make a winter shelter for the ladybugs in your garden out of an old plastic planter (a 1-gallon-sized pot works well). Cut a 1-inch square near the top rim. This will be the "door" to your ladybug house. Find a protected grassy area in your backyard. Mist the grass with a little water. Add several leaves. Flip the pot over, and place it firmly on the grass over the leaves (put a few rocks on top to weigh it down). Your ladybug house is now ready for its winter guests!

Beetles are one of nature's most amazing success stories. They have lived on our planet for hundreds of millions of years. From the hard-working dung beetle to the clever lightning bug, these tiny creatures are fun and educational to watch. We are just beginning to learn all they have to teach us about surviving and thriving in a changing world.

# Glossary

**basking**     resting while also soaking up heat from the sun

**carrion**     dead animals

**cocoon**     a silky covering spun by insects to protect them while they are in the pupa stage

**dung**     the solid waste produced by an animal

**elytra**     the two hard covers that protect a beetle's hind wings

**exoskeleton**     the hard outer covering of an insect that provides support and protection for the body

**field marks**     spots, stripes, or other distinguishing marks on an animal

**larva**     the feeding stage of a young insect

**luminescent**     giving off light from the body by producing a natural chemical

**mandibles**     the strong lower jaws of an insect

**nectar**     a sweet liquid secreted by flowers

**pheromones**     chemicals released by insects that allow them to communicate with each other

**pollen**     a fine, powdery substance produced by plants, necessary for their reproduction

**pupa**     an insect in a nonfeeding, inactive stage as it changes from larva to adult

# Find Out More

## Books

Kenney, Karen Latchana. *Hide with the Ladybugs.* Minneapolis, MN: Magic Wagon, 2010.
Sexton, Colleen. *The Life Cycle of a Ladybug.* Minneapolis, MN: Bellwether Media, 2010.
Woodward, John. *Beetles.* New York: Chelsea Clubhouse, 2010.

## Websites

**BioKids Critter Catalog: Beetles**
www.biokids.umich.edu/critters/Coleoptera
See photos and discover interesting facts about numerous North American beetle species, from click beetles to tiger beetles.

**National Geographic**
http://animals.nationalgeographic.com/animals/bugs.html
Visit to read about scarabs, ladybugs, lightning bugs, and other colorful beetles from around the world. Watch videos of beetles in action.

**Scarabs for Kids**
www.museum.unl.edu/research/entomology/Scarabs-for-Kids/home.html
Here you can explore the lives of scarabs, some of the most beautiful and valuable beetles in the world. This site, sponsored by the University of Nebraska State Museum, also features fun activities for kids.

# Index

Page numbers in **boldface** are illustrations.

basking, 27
beetle guide, 20–23
benefits and damage
  of beetles, 24
body structure, 9–11, **10**

carrion, 24
click beetles, 9
cocoons, 7–8

darkling beetles, 17
dung, 6
dung beetle, **9**, 11

eggs, 6, **6**
elytra, 9, **9**
exoskeleton, 8

field marks, 17

habitat, 11, 14–15
Hercules beetle, 12, **12**
hind wings, 9, **9**

identifying beetles, 20–23

ladybugs, 5, **5**, 7, **7**, 15,
  **15**, 26–28
larva, 6, 7, **7**
life cycle, 6–8
light, attraction to, 25
lightning bugs, 25, **25**
luminescent, 25

mandibles, **10**, 11

nectar, 11

pheromones, 10
pollen, 24
pupa, 6, 7, **8**

scarab beetle, 24
soldier beetle, **8**

tiger beetle, 14, **14**
tumblebug, 6, 11

# About the Author

**TRUDI STRAIN TRUEIT** has written more than seventy-five nonfiction books for young readers, covering topics such as weather, wildlife, health, and history. She is the author of nine other books in the Backyard Safari series, including *Ants, Dragonflies,* and *Grasshoppers.* Trueit lives in Everett, Washington, with her husband, Bill, a high school photography teacher. Visit her website at www.truditrueit.com.